Wolfgang Amadeus Mozart

REQUIEM

IN FULL SCORE

Dover Publications, Inc.

NEW YORK

Published in Canada by General Publishing Company, Ltd.,
30 Lesmill Road, Don Mills, Toronto, Ontario.
Published in the United Kingdom by Constable and Company,
Ltd., 10 Orange Street, London WC2H 7EG.

This Dover edition, first published in 1987,
is an unabridged republication of the work originally published
by Breitkopf & Härtel, Wiesbaden, n.d., with the title
Mozart, Requiem für vier Singstimmen, Orchester und Orgel.
A table of contents and a table of instruments
and voices have been added.

Manufactured in the United States of America
Dover Publications, Inc., 31 East 2nd Street, Mineola, N.Y. 11501

Library of Congress Cataloging in Publication Data

Mozart, Wolfgang Amadeus, 1756–1791.
[Requiem, K. 626, D minor. Latin]
Requiem.

In full score.
For solo voices (SATB), chorus (SATB), and orchestra.
Reprint. Originally published: Wiesbaden :
Breitkopf & Härtel, n.d.
1. Requiems—scores.
M2010.M93K.626   1987   86-753798
ISBN 0-486-25311-2

Contents

Instruments and Voices

Mozart left the *Requiem*, K.626, unfinished at his death in 1791.
It was completed by Franz Xaver Süssmayr (1766–1803).
Their respective contributions are indicated in the score
by the initials (M.) and (S.).

2 Corni di Bassetto (F)
2 Fagotti

Coro: Soprani
      Alti
      Tenori
      Bassi

2 Trombe (D, B)
3 Tromboni (Alto, Tenore e Basso)

Violini I
Violini II

Timpani (D, A)

Viole
Violoncelli

Organo

Contrabassi

Soprano solo
Alto solo
Tenore solo
Basso solo

Requiem

Dies irae

Tuba mirum

Rex tremendae

dae, Rex tre_men_dae ma_jes_ta_tis, qui salvan_dos salvas gra_tis;

Rex tre_men_dae ma_jes_ta_tis, qui salvan_dos salvas gra_tis;

_dae, Rex tre_men_dae ma_jes_ta_tis, qui salvan_dos salvas gra_tis;

men_dae, Rex tre_men_dae ma_jes_ta_tis, qui salvan_dos salvas gra_tis;

SOLO

tasto

Recordare

Confutatis

ge _ re cu _ ram me _ i fi _ _ _ _ nis!

ge _ re cu _ ram me _ i fi _ _ _ _ nis!

cu _ _ ram me _ i fi _ _ _ _ nis!

Lacrimosa

Hu ic er go par ce, De us, pi e Je su, Je su, Do mi ne!

Domine Jesu

Hostias

Corni di Bassetto (S.)		Andante (S.)
Fagotti (S.)		(Senza Tromboni.)
Violino I		(M.) (S.)
Violino II		(M.) (S.)
Viola		(M.) (S.)
Soprano (M.)		TUTTI
Alto (M.)		TUTTI
Tenore (M.)		TUTTI
Basso (M.)		TUTTI
Violoncello Basso ed Organo (M.)		SOLO TUTTI

si_sti, quam o_lim A_brahae pro_mi_si_____sti, et se_____mi_ni e_____jus.

si_sti, quam o_lim A_brahae pro_mi_si_____sti, et se_mi_ni, se_mi_ni e_____jus.

si_sti, quam o_lim A_brahae pro_mi_si_____sti, et se_mi_ni, se_mi_ni e_____jus.

quam o_lim A_brahae pro_mi _ si_sti, pro_mi_si____sti, et se_mi_ni, se_mi_ni e____jus.

Ho_sti_as et pre_ces ti_bi, Do_mi_ne, ti_bi,

Ho_sti_as et pre_ces ti_bi, Do_mi_ne, ti_bi,

Andante (S.)

64

Sanctus

74

Benedictus

67

sis! O _ san _ _ na in ex _ cel _ _ _ sis! O _ san _ na in ex _ cel _ _ sis!

_ _ _ sis! O _ san _ _ na in ex _ cel _ sis! O _ san _ na in ex _ cel _ sis!

_ _ _ _ sis! O _ san _ na in _ ex _ cel _ sis, in _ ex _ cel _ sis!

san _ na in _ ex _ cel _ _ _ _ _ _ sis! O _ san _ na in ex _ cel _ _ sis!

Agnus Dei